# Let's Real

# About Suicide

*"Facing Life After Suicide Loss"*

A Guide for Families, Friends & Community:
How to Survive & Be There After the Loss

COPYRIGHT © Melissa M Bottorff-Arey, 2023
ALL RIGHTS RESERVED.
Please respect the many hours and expertise that went into putting this complimentary guide together. Any sharing, copying, or reproduction without consent of any kind is very strictly prohibited. We will gladly provide this resource by request. Thank you.

*"What we have once enjoyed
& deeply loved
we can never lose,
for all that we love deeply
becomes a part of us."*
— Helen Keller

www.theleftoverpieces.com/resources

# *This is beyond hard*

Start by writing their name...

_____

Date of Birth  _____/_____/_____

Date of Loss  _____/_____/_____

> *"Though you left*
> *this world behind that day,*
> *you still live on through*
> *your place in my heart."*
> *– J.Betts*

*This guide is written BY a survivor mom,*
*FOR survivors everywhere, with love.*

"The pain you hid
overtook you
like the darkness overtakes
the sun.
But I comfort myself
in knowing that
even on the darkest night,
stars still shine."

# *Suicide. But WHY??*

Suicide is very complicated. Understanding mental health is also. Our brain can play tricks on us when it is ill. ANYONE can suffer from mental illness. Some illness is acute (short term, like a cold) & some is chronic (long lasting, requiring treatment). But, unrecognized (untreated) the result can be devastating, & even life ending. It was not their fault.

## *Is suicide selfish?*
## *Not even a little. Their mind broke.*

They were probably full of life. Perhaps their struggle was long, or maybe no one saw any signs. Suicide does not discriminate or have a 'type'. Most people that die by suicide just want the pain in their mind to end. They were an amazing person. It probably was not about dying. They loved & cared for you - their friends & family - & they knew they were loved. Their mind was not functioning correctly, even to the point that it tricked them into thinking false thoughts. They would never have caused this kind of hurt intentionally. Trust that this is true. Again, suicide is very complicated.

*"If you've lost a loved one to suicide
—even if you, yourself,
have dealt with depression
and suicidal ideation
—you may often wonder why.
And that's okay.
Allow yourself that space."*

– K. Espenshade

# Feeling Guilty?

Wondering what you could have said, or done, that might have prevented your loved one's suicide is normal. There is so much we don't know about what other people are going through. Chances are, they simply didn't know how to reach out & ask for help.

Guilt comes when we have feelings that we have done something wrong. It often comes out in self-anger. You did not do anything wrong that caused your loved one's feelings, or actions. Anger toward yourself is misplaced & not productive in healing.

*I just keep thinking
& wondering & wishing;
plagued by the what-ifs & the if-onlys.*

Having feelings of guilt (& anger) will be part of suicide grief but be sure to give yourself permission to do just that, grieve, which will include feeling ALL of the emotions, even guilt & anger.

# How to Support Loss Survivors

## SAY. THEIR. NAME.

Say it often. This is what keeps their memory alive. Talking about them is a good thing.

This is one of the most helpful things you can do. Truly. Suicide loss survivors overwhelmingly agree that they need people to TALK about their loved one. They want them to be remembered...forever.

### *But I don't want to make them sad by talking about them.*

You won't make them sad. They are sad...naturally. You are probably very sad too. That's part of loss. Feeling our emotions (all of them) is not only normal, but it's healthy. It's ok to feel your way through this & it's ok to lean on each other. Not talking about them only makes their friends & family feel lonely... & like their loved one didn't matter to others.

Simply ignoring grievers to "give them space" is not a good thing for them, that's really more for you...challenge yourself to step into your discomfort to be there for them. We cannot do this alone.

# What to Say - What NOT to Say

It's about how it makes them FEEL, not what you intend

## Say things like...

- "How are you holding up today?" or "How's today?"
- "I have no idea what to say, but I will sit with you."
- "This really sucks... "I cannot imagine how hard this is and I am so sorry that you are living through this."
- "You can talk to me about (name) - anytime."

*I would go see them, or call, but I don't know what to say...*

## Don't say things such as...

- A casual "Hey, how are you?" (which often feels dismissive, not supportive)
- Don't ask anything about method/specifics.(Period)
- "Time will heal." (it doesn't, it takes work)
- "Everything happens for a reason." (just no)
- "They wouldn't want you to be sad." (too bad)
- "They're in a better place." (they should be here)
- "I understand how you feel." (even if it seems similar, we all have unique feelings about loss)

## BUT, Before Saying Anything...

Ask yourself, *"Is this helpful?"*
If it's not, simply saying
*"I don't know what to say, but I'm here"*, is better.

*"That's the thing about suicide. Try as you might to remember how a person lived his life, you always end up thinking about how they ended it."* – Anderson Cooper

# *The Days & Weeks Ahead*

## What the family needs in the first days & weeks

- Give space as needed. Be respectful of boundaries.
- Take food &/or help organize a meal train.
- Drop-off household goods - like paper goods, snacks, water, or gift cards for meals or groceries.
- Donate toward final expenses if appropriate.
- Offer to organize a donation campaign with the family's permission.
- Take their laundry 1x a week.(or setup a rotation with friends, like meals).
- Text from store to see if you can grab anything.

## *I want to help, but what can I do?*

- Check in on them with texts or calls. Continue to try, even if they don't respond. Some days are bad & some better - sometimes a message is enough.
- If you can, just do things like mow the yard, clean the house or even walk the dog(s).
- Run carpool for them or help with their other kids.
- Share memories, & pictures, & stories. (on-going)
- Be willing to just sit with them. Let them talk, cry or sit in silence. Their needs will vary day to day.

# *In the Years to Come*

## How to help the family in the first year:

- Put the important dates (birthday, loss day, etc.) in your calendar & reach out to family on those days just to acknowledge you care. It will matter a lot.
- Take them to lunch or bring lunch (or coffee) to them if they don't want to get out.
- Around the ONE YEAR date - reach out & offer extra support - they will need it & may not ask.

## In the years that lay ahead:

- Keep the dates in your calendar. They need someone to remember with them, yes, EVERY year.
- Talk about their loved one, share stories & photos. ASK their friends & family how they are doing. It matters more than you think.

### *It's been a year; do I still reach out?*
### *Yes, resoundingly, YES!*

Suicide loss devastates; it shatters the world of the family left behind. This is more than loss, it's trauma, & you do not just move on. It takes a lot of support & work to learn to live alongside this grief. You don't get over it, but you can move forward --- eventually.

*"No matter what people tell you, words and ideas can change the world."*
–Robin Williams

# What Can I Do for Suicide Loss & Mental Health Awareness?

## There are things you can do TODAY

- Go to AFSP.com & find out when the next community walk in your area is. Help organize a team in honor of the loved one you have lost (include the family if possible).
- Volunteer for NAMI or a local group to encourage mental health empowerment.

*What do I know anyway? One person can't really make a difference ...or, can they?*

## Think ripple effect...

- Wear a bracelet, or a tee-shirt, or heck, get a memorial tattoo...these are good memorials but also serve as great conversation starters.
- Be willing to have hard conversations (even with strangers) to educate & stop the stigma.
- See the 'Resources' link in this booklet for more.

*Be brave enough  
to start a conversation  
that matters.*  
– M. Wheatley

# What Can I Do at Home?
## Having Mental Health Empowerment Conversations on the Daily

- Make your own mental health a priority. Lead by example - it matters. YOU matter.
- Check on your 'strong' friends, your 'happy' friends, & yes, your 'struggling' friends.
- Ask hard questions and be willing to listen to the answers. Listen to really hear, not just to respond.

> *"What mental health needs is more sunlight, more candor, & more unashamed conversation."*
> – Glenn Close

- Seek out books, podcasts, courses...anything you can find on suicide loss & grief. Education is power.
- Plan a regular time (weekly) to discuss your feelings as a family - meals can be a good time.
- If someone is at risk or says they're struggling, it's ok to ask if they feel suicidal. It empowers them to trust you if they feel like there is no shame in admitting it. Dial 988 - the Crisis Lifeline if needed.

# *Allow Space for Grief.*

Know that grief is normal.

---

Look for online & in-person support groups.

---

Grief is not linear & does not have a timeline.
You learn to live alongside it. It doesn't go away.

### ♡ *How **long** does grief last, & will I need support...?*

We all grieve differently - allow for that.

---

Eliminate 'extras' in your schedule - make space.

---

Try to keep routines as normal as possible.
Eat, drink water & get rest.

# *And Give Yourself a Lot of Grace*

You can laugh, even feel happy, AND be grieving.

———

Get outside. Move your body. (It really helps).

———

Journal. Meditate. Listen to music. Dance.

———

See a therapist, doctor or experts for extra support. Asking for help is always ok.

*Give yourself extra space  
& plenty of grace when grieving  
...this is hard work.*

# Helpful Spaces for All
## A Podcast for anyone grieving after suicide loss

www.theleftoverpieces.com/resources

# Helpful Spaces for All
There are so many resources here, all with links

www.theleftoverpieces.com/resources

## *NOTES:*

Write down ideas you may have to help, or things you want to remember. You will be surprised how thankful you are later that you took the time to make notes. Write down names of family or friends (including phone #'s) that you may want to recall or connect with at a later date.

_____
_____
_____
_____
_____
_____
_____
_____
_____
_____
_____
_____
_____
_____

Need Help? Call 988 Suicide & Crisis Lifeline

www.theleftoverpieces.com

"Never say goodbye,
because saying goodbye
means going away
and going away
means forgetting."
-Peter Pan

& no one here is
ever forgetting

Made in the USA
Columbia, SC
06 January 2025